40 Favorite Impossible Pies

Main Dishes & Desserts

Gloria Hander Lyons

Blue Sage Press

40 Favorite Impossible Pies
Main Dishes & Desserts

Inquires should be addressed to:
Blue Sage Press
48 Borondo Pines
La Marque, TX 77568
www.BlueSagePress.com

ISBN: 978-0-9802244-7-4

Library of Congress Control Number: 2009903283

First Edition: April 2009

Printed in the United States of America

Table of Contents

Pies Made with Ham & Pork

Ham & Broccoli Casserole Pie
Pork & Hominy Pie
Pork Stroganoff Pie
Pork Tamale Pie
Scalloped Potato & Ham Pie

Pies Made with Vegetables

Fiesta Black Bean Pie
Green Bean Casserole Pie
Macaroni & Cheese Pie
Sweet Potato Casserole Pie
Zucchini & Tomato Pie

Impossible Dessert Pies

Apple Pie
Buttermilk Pie
Brownie Pie
Cheesecake Pie
Chocolate Cream Pie
Coconut Custard Pie
Lemon Custard Pie
Peaches & Cream Pie
Pecan Pie
Pumpkin Pie

40 Favorite Impossible Pies

Introduction

If you're not familiar with the concept of the "Impossible Pie", you're in for a real treat. These quick and easy entrees and desserts are shaped like a pie, but without all the fuss involved with making a traditional pie crust with a filling.

Impossible pies were first invented during the 1970s by home economists at the General Mills Corporation. They used Bisquick® baking mix, milk and eggs to create a batter that was poured over sweet or savory ingredients in a pie plate. The pie formed its own "crust" while baking and the finished product was then cut into pie-shaped wedges.

American cooks have since created hundreds of variations of the original impossible pie recipes. I've included 40 of my favorites in this book, like Philly Cheese Steak Pie, Turkey Club Pie, Tuna Casserole Pie and Scalloped Potato & Ham Pie.

Once you know the basic formula for making these simple main dish pies (page 2), you can create your own versions. Each pie makes six regular or four large servings. You can store the leftovers in the refrigerator for several days or in the freezer for up to 3 months; then reheat in a microwave oven for a quick lunch or dinner meal.

These tasty meat pies are great for packing in your lunch box and reheating in the microwave at work.

1

Basic Formula For Making Main Dish Pies

Most of the main dish impossible pie recipes in this book are made using the following basic formula and baked in a 9" X 1-1/2" glass pie plate.

For the batter, whisk together:
    1 cup milk
    2 large eggs
    1/2 cup Bisquick® baking mix

Add various seasonings of your choice to the batter, like salt, pepper, garlic powder, herbs or other dry seasonings.

You can also substitute other liquids, like tomato sauce or barbecue sauce, for part of the milk to change the flavor of the pie.

For the filling, use a combination of some or all of the following to equal approximately 3-1/2 to 4 cups:
    1-1/2 to 2 cups cooked meat
    1/2 to 1 cup vegetables
    1 cup shredded cheese (or substitute cooked rice or
        mashed potato)

To make a lighter version of your main dish pie, substitute some or all of the following: skim milk, low fat cheese, egg whites or egg substitute and Bisquick® Heart Smart baking mix.

Each of the main dish pie recipes makes a hearty, budget-conscious meal your family will love. I've also included ten dessert pie recipes that are not only quick and easy, but scrumptious!

You'll want to try them all!

Impossible Pies
Made with
Bacon & Sausage

Impossible BLT Pie

14-16 slices bacon, cooked & crumbled (about 1 cup)
1/2 cup chopped tomato (fresh or canned, well drained)
1 cup shredded Swiss cheese (or cheese of your choice)
3/4 cup Bisquick® baking mix
1 cup milk
1/4 cup mayonnaise
3 large eggs
1/4 teaspoon salt
1/8 teaspoon pepper

Preheat oven to 400°. Spray a 9" X 1-1/2" glass pie plate with cooking spray.

Mix together bacon, tomato and cheese. Spread mixture in pie plate.

In a small bowl, stir remaining ingredients together with a wire whisk until well blended. Pour into pie plate.

Bake 35-40 minutes or until knife inserted in center comes out clean. Let stand at least 10 minutes before serving.

Top each slice with chopped lettuce and tomato or serve with a tossed green salad on the side.

Impossible Sausage Breakfast Pie

1 pound bulk pork sausage
1/2 cup chopped green pepper
1/2 cup chopped onion
1 cup grated Cheddar cheese (4 oz.)
1/2 cup Bisquick® baking mix
1 cup milk
2 large eggs
1/4 teaspoon salt
1/8 teaspoon pepper

Preheat oven to 400°. Spray a 9" X 1-1/2" glass pie plate with cooking spray.

In a skillet, cook sausage, onion and green pepper until done; drain fat. Let cool slightly and stir in cheese. Spread mixture in pie plate.

In a small bowl, beat remaining ingredients together with a wire whisk until well blended. Pour into pie plate.

Bake 35-40 minutes or until knife inserted in center comes out clean. Let stand 10 minutes before serving.

Serve warm with a side of fresh fruit.

Impossible Sauerkraut & Sausage Pie

2 cups diced smoked link sausage
1/4 cup chopped onion
1 cup canned sauerkraut, rinsed & well drained
1 cup shredded Swiss cheese
1/2 cup Bisquick® baking mix
1 cup milk
2 large eggs
1/4 teaspoon salt
Pinch of ground black pepper

Preheat oven to 400°. Spray a 9" X 1-1/2" glass pie plate with cooking spray.

In a skillet, cook sausage with onion until onion is tender; drain fat. Let cool slightly. Stir in sauerkraut and cheese. Spread mixture in pie plate.

In a small bowl, beat remaining ingredients together with a wire whisk until well blended. Pour into pie plate.

Bake 35-40 minutes or until knife inserted in center comes out clean. Let stand at least 10 minutes before serving.

Impossible Sausage, Red Beans & Rice Pie

1 cup smoked pork link sausage, diced
1/4 cup chopped onion
1/4 cup chopped celery
1 (15 oz.) can red kidney beans, well drained
1 cup cooked white rice (use left-over rice if you have it*)
1/2 cup Bisquick® baking mix
1/4 teaspoon garlic powder
1/2 teaspoon salt
Pinch of ground black pepper
Dash of hot sauce (to taste)
1 cup milk
2 large eggs

Preheat oven to 400°. Spray a 9" X 1-1/2" glass pie plate with cooking spray.

In a skillet, cook sausage with onion and celery until vegetables are tender; drain fat. Stir in beans and rice. Spread mixture in pie plate.

In a small bowl, beat remaining ingredients together with a wire whisk until well blended. Pour into pie plate.

Bake 35-40 minutes or until knife inserted in center comes out clean. Let stand 10 minutes before serving.

Serve with a side of coleslaw.

*Other recipes in this cookbook that call for cooked white rice: Tuna Polynesia Pie (page 26), Ham & Broccoli Casserole Pie (page 28) and Pork Stroganoff Pie (page 32).

Impossible Sausage & Pepperoni Pizza Pie

1/2 pound bulk pork sausage
1/4 cup chopped green pepper
1/4 cup chopped onion
1/2 cup chopped, canned tomatoes, well drained
1/2 cup shredded Mozzarella cheese
1/2 cup Bisquick® baking mix
3/4 cup milk
2 large eggs
1/2 teaspoon dried oregano leaves
1/2 teaspoon dried, crushed basil leaves
1/4 teaspoon garlic powder
1/4 teaspoon salt
1 cup shredded Mozzarella cheese
18-20 thin slices pepperoni

Preheat oven to 400º. Spray a 9" X 1-1/2" glass pie plate with cooking spray.

In a skillet, cook sausage, onion and green pepper until done. Drain fat and stir in tomatoes. Spread mixture in pie plate.

Sprinkle with 1/2 cup Mozzarella cheese.

In a small bowl, beat baking mix, milk, eggs, oregano, basil, garlic powder and salt together with a wire whisk until well blended. Pour into pie plate.

Bake 25 minutes. Remove from oven and top with remaining 1 cup cheese and pepperoni slices. Bake for another 10-15 minutes or until top is lightly browned and knife inserted in center comes out clean. Let stand at least 10 minutes before serving.

Impossible Pies Made with Beef

Impossible Cheeseburger Pie

1 lb. ground sirloin or lean ground beef
1/2 cup chopped onion
1 cup shredded Cheddar cheese (4 oz.)
1/2 cup Bisquick® baking mix
3/4 cup milk
3 tablespoons catsup
1 tablespoon prepared mustard
2 large eggs
1/2 teaspoon salt
Pinch of ground black pepper

Preheat oven to 400°. Spray a 9" X 1-1/2" glass pie plate with cooking spray.

In a skillet, cook beef and onion until done; drain. Let cool slightly. Stir in cheese and spread mixture in pie plate.

In a small bowl, beat remaining ingredients together with a wire whisk until well blended. Pour into pie plate.

Bake 25-30 minutes or until knife inserted in center comes out clean. Let stand at least 10 minutes before serving.

Top each slice with chopped lettuce and tomato and serve with a side of French fried potatoes.

Impossible Beef Taco Pie

1 lb. ground sirloin or lean ground beef
1/2 cup chopped onion
1/2 cup chunky salsa
2 teaspoons taco seasoning mix
1/2 cup coarsely crushed tortilla chips
  (a 1-oz. bag of Cool Ranch flavor Doritos works well)
1 cup shredded Cheddar cheese, divided
1/2 cup Bisquick® baking mix
3/4 cup milk
2 large eggs
1/4 teaspoon salt
Lettuce and tomato

Preheat oven to 400°. Spray a 9" X 1-1/2" glass pie plate with cooking spray.

In a skillet, cook beef and onion until done. Drain and stir in salsa, taco seasoning, tortilla chips and 1/2 cup cheese. Spread mixture in pie plate.

In a small bowl, beat baking mix, milk, eggs and salt together with a wire whisk until well blended. Pour into pie plate.

Bake 35-40 minutes or until knife inserted in center comes out clean. Sprinkle with remaining 1/2 cup cheese and return to oven for a couple of minutes until cheese is melted. Let stand 10 minutes before serving.

Top each slice with chopped lettuce and tomato and serve with extra salsa if desired.

Impossible Meatloaf & Mashed Potato Pie

1 lb. ground sirloin or lean ground beef
1/2 cup chopped onion
1/2 cup chopped celery
1 cup cooked potato, peeled and mashed*
1/2 cup Bisquick® baking mix
1 cup milk
2 large eggs
1/4 teaspoon garlic powder
1/2 teaspoon salt
Pinch of ground black pepper
Optional: 1/2 cup tomato sauce or catsup

Preheat oven to 400°. Spray a 9" X 1-1/2" glass pie plate with cooking spray.

In a skillet, cook beef, onion and celery until done; drain. Stir in potato and spread mixture in pie plate.

In a small bowl, beat baking mix, milk, eggs, garlic powder, salt and pepper, using a wire whisk until well blended. Pour into pie plate.

Bake 35-40 minutes or until knife inserted in center comes out clean. Optional: Remove pie from oven after baking for 30 minutes. Spread 1/2 cup tomato sauce or catsup over top and return to oven for another 5-10 minutes or until done. Let stand 10 minutes before serving.

*Cook a medium-size potato in the microwave until soft. Let cool slightly, then peel and mash.

Impossible Barbecue Beef Pie

1 lb. ground sirloin or lean ground beef
1/4 cup chopped onion
1/4 cup chopped green pepper
1 (11 oz.) can Pork 'n Beans, well drained
1/2 cup Bisquick® baking mix
3/4 cup milk
1/4 cup barbecue sauce
2 large eggs
1/2 teaspoon salt
Pinch of ground black pepper

Preheat oven to 400º. Spray a 9" X 1-1/2" glass pie plate with cooking spray.

In a skillet, cook beef, onion and green pepper until done; drain. Stir in beans and spread mixture in pie plate.

In a small bowl, beat remaining ingredients together with a wire whisk until well blended. Pour into pie plate.

Bake 35-40 minutes or until knife inserted in center comes out clean. Let stand 10 minutes before serving.

Serve warm with a side of potato salad or coleslaw.

Impossible Philly Cheese Steak Pie

2 cups left-over cooked & chopped roast beef
   (You can also use deli roast beef, about 1/2 lb.)
1/2 cup finely chopped onion
1/2 cup finely chopped green pepper
1 cup shredded Provolone cheese (or cheese of your choice)
1/2 cup Bisquick® baking mix
1 cup milk
2 large eggs
1/2 teaspoon salt
Pinch of ground black pepper

Preheat oven to 400°. Spray a 9" X 1-1/2" glass pie plate with cooking spray.

Mix together beef, onion, green pepper and cheese. Spread in pie plate.

In a small bowl, beat remaining ingredients together with a wire whisk until well blended. Pour into pie plate.

Bake 35-40 minutes or until knife inserted in center comes out clean. Let stand 10 minutes before serving.

Serve warm with a tossed green salad or side of fresh fruit.

Impossible Pies Made with Chicken & Turkey

Impossible Chicken Quesadilla Pie

2 cups chopped, cooked chicken
1/2 cup finely chopped onion
1 (4 oz.) can chopped green chilies, well drained
1-1/2 cups shredded Monterey Jack cheese (6 oz.)
    (or use Colby/Monterey Jack)
1/2 cup Bisquick® baking mix
1 cup milk
2 large eggs
1/2 teaspoon salt
1/4 teaspoon garlic powder

Preheat oven to 400°. Spray a 9" X 1-1/2" glass pie plate with cooking spray.

Mix together chicken, onion, green chilies and cheese. Spread mixture in pie plate.

In a small bowl, beat remaining ingredients together with a wire whisk until well blended. Pour into pie plate.

Bake 35-40 minutes or until knife inserted in center comes out clean. Let stand 10 minutes before serving.

Serve warm with a tossed green salad or sour cream and salsa if desired.

Impossible Chicken Pot Pie

1-1/2 cups chopped, cooked chicken
1 cup frozen peas and carrots, thawed and well drained
1 cup cooked potato, peeled and diced*
1/2 cup finely chopped onion
1 teaspoon chicken bouillon granules
1/2 cup Bisquick® baking mix
1 cup milk
2 large eggs
1/4 teaspoon salt
Pinch of ground black pepper

Preheat oven to 400°. Spray a 9" X 1-1/2" glass pie plate with cooking spray.

Stir together chicken, peas and carrots, potato, onion and bouillon. Spread mixture in pie plate.

In a small bowl, beat remaining ingredients together with a wire whisk until well blended. Pour into pie plate.

Bake 35-40 minutes or until knife inserted in center comes out clean. Let stand 10 minutes before serving.

*Cook a medium-size potato in the microwave until soft. Let cool slightly, then peel and dice.

Impossible Turkey Ranch Pie

2 cups chopped, cooked turkey (or chicken)
1 cup frozen mixed vegetables, thawed and well drained
1 cup shredded Monterey Jack cheese (4 oz.)
1 envelope (1 oz.) ranch dressing mix
1/2 cup Bisquick® baking mix
1 cup milk
2 large eggs
1/4 teaspoon salt
Pinch of ground black pepper

Preheat oven to 400°. Spray a 9" X 1-1/2" glass pie plate with cooking spray.

Mix together turkey, vegetables and cheese. Spread mixture in pie plate.

In a small bowl, beat remaining ingredients together with a wire whisk until well blended. Pour into pie plate.

Bake 35-40 minutes or until knife inserted in center comes out clean. Let stand 10 minutes before serving.

Impossible Turkey Club Pie

2 cups chopped, cooked turkey (or chicken)
8 slices bacon, cooked & crumbled (about 1/2 cup)
1 cup shredded Cheddar cheese (4 oz.)
1/2 cup Bisquick® baking mix
1 cup milk
2 large eggs
1/4 teaspoon salt
Pinch of ground black pepper

Preheat oven to 400°. Spray a 9" X 1-1/2" glass pie plate with cooking spray.

Mix together turkey, bacon and cheese. Spread in pie plate.

In a small bowl, beat remaining ingredients together with a wire whisk until well blended. Pour into pie plate.

Bake 35-40 minutes or until knife inserted in center comes out clean. Let stand 10 minutes before serving.

Serve warm with a tossed green salad or side of fresh fruit.

Impossible Thanksgiving Dinner Pie

1/4 cup chopped celery
1/4 cup chopped onion
2 cups chopped, cooked turkey (or chicken)
1 cup dry stuffing mix for turkey or chicken
1/2 cup hot water
1 teaspoon instant chicken bouillon granules
1 cup milk
1/2 cup Bisquick® baking mix
2 large eggs
1/4 teaspoon salt
Pinch of ground black pepper
1/2 teaspoon poultry seasoning (optional)
1/2 teaspoon ground dried sage (optional)

Preheat oven to 400°. Spray a 9" X 1-1/2" glass pie plate with cooking spray.

In a skillet, sauté onion and celery in a small amount of vegetable oil until tender. Stir in turkey and stuffing mix. Spread mixture in pie plate.

In a small bowl, dissolve bouillon in 1/2 cup hot water. Add remaining ingredients and beat using a wire whisk until well blended. Pour into pie plate.

Bake 35-40 minutes or until knife inserted in center comes out clean. Let stand 10 minutes before serving.

Serve warm with cranberry sauce.

Impossible Pies
Made with
Fish
& Seafood

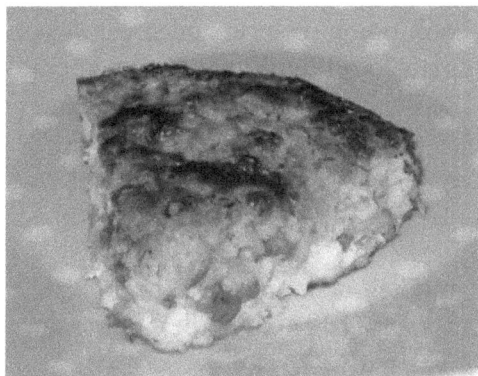

Impossible Crab Cake Pie

1/4 cup chopped onion
1/4 cup chopped celery
1/4 cup chopped green bell pepper
2 (6 oz.) cans crab meat, well drained and flaked
3/4 cup fresh bread crumbs*
1 cup Cheddar cheese
1/2 cup Bisquick® baking mix
1 cup milk
2 large eggs
1/2 teaspoon salt
Pinch of ground black pepper
1/2 teaspoon Worcestershire sauce
1 teaspoon lemon juice
Hot sauce to taste (optional)

Preheat oven to 400°. Spray a 9" X 1-1/2" glass pie plate with cooking spray.

In a skillet, cook onion, celery, and green pepper in a small amount of vegetable oil until tender. Stir in crab meat, bread crumbs and cheese. Spread mixture in pie plate.

In a small bowl, beat remaining ingredients together with a wire whisk until well blended. Pour into pie plate.

Bake 35-40 minutes or until knife inserted in center comes out clean. Let stand 10 minutes before serving. Serve with tartar sauce if desired.

*To make bread crumbs, tear two slices of bread into large pieces and process in a blender or food processor.

Impossible Salmon Pie

2 (5 oz.) cans boneless, skinless salmon, drained and flaked
1-1/2 cups cooked potato, peeled and chopped*
1/4 cup finely chopped onion
1 (2 oz.) jar chopped pimiento, well drained
1 cup shredded Cheddar cheese
1 teaspoon dried dill weed
1/2 cup Bisquick® baking mix
1 cup milk
2 large eggs
1/2 teaspoon salt
Pinch of ground black pepper

Preheat oven to 400°. Spray a 9" X 1-1/2" glass pie plate with cooking spray.

Mix together salmon, potato, onion, pimiento, cheese and dill. Spread mixture in pie plate.

In a small bowl, beat remaining ingredients together with a wire whisk until well blended. Pour into pie plate.

Bake 35-40 minutes or until knife inserted in center comes out clean. Let stand 10 minutes before serving.

*Cook two medium-size potatoes in the microwave until soft. Let cool slightly, then peel and chop.

Impossible Tuna Casserole Pie

2 (5 oz.) cans solid Albacore tuna, drained and flaked
1-1/4 cups crushed potato chips (about 2 oz.)
3/4 cup frozen green peas, thawed and well drained
1 cup shredded Cheddar cheese (4 oz.)
1/4 cup finely chopped onion
1/2 cup Bisquick® baking mix
1 cup milk
2 large eggs
1/4 teaspoon salt
Pinch of ground black pepper

Preheat oven to 400º. Spray a 9" X 1-1/2" glass pie plate with cooking spray.

Mix together tuna, potato chips, peas, cheese and onion. Spread mixture in pie plate.

In a small bowl, beat remaining ingredients together with a wire whisk until well blended. Pour into pie plate.

Bake 35-40 minutes or until knife inserted in center comes out clean. Let stand 10 minutes before serving.

Impossible Shrimp & Cheese Pie

2 (6 oz.) cans tiny shrimp, well drained
1 cup frozen green peas, thawed and well drained
1/4 cup finely chopped onion
1 cup grated Swiss cheese (or cheese of your choice)
1/2 cup Bisquick® baking mix
1 cup milk
2 large eggs
1/2 teaspoon salt
1/2 teaspoon dried thyme
Pinch of ground black pepper

Preheat oven to 400°. Spray a 9" X 1-1/2" glass pie plate with cooking spray.

Mix together shrimp, peas, onion and cheese. Spread mixture in pie plate.

In a small bowl, beat remaining ingredients together with a wire whisk until well blended. Pour into pie plate.

Bake 35-40 minutes or until knife inserted in center comes out clean. Let stand 10 minutes before serving.

Impossible Tuna Polynesia Pie

2 (5 oz.) cans solid Albacore tuna, drained and flaked
1 cup cooked white rice (use left-over rice if you have it*)
1 (8 oz.) can crushed pineapple, undrained
1/2 cup sliced almonds**
1/4 cup finely chopped onion
1/4 cup finely chopped green bell pepper
1/2 cup Bisquick® baking mix
1/3 cup milk
1/2 cup condensed cream of mushroom soup
2 large eggs
1/2 teaspoon salt
Pinch of ground black pepper

Preheat oven to 400°. Spray a 9" X 1-1/2" glass pie plate with cooking spray.

Mix together tuna, rice, pineapple, almonds, onion and green pepper. Spread mixture in pie plate.

In a small bowl, beat remaining ingredients together with a wire whisk until well blended. Pour into pie plate.

Bake 35-40 minutes or until knife inserted in center comes out clean. Let stand 10 minutes before serving.

*Other recipes in this cookbook that call for cooked white rice: Sausage, Red Beans & Rice Pie (page 7), Ham & Broccoli Casserole Pie (page 28) and Pork Stroganoff Pie (page 32).

**For added flavor, toast the almonds in a dry skillet over medium-high heat for 3-4 minutes, stirring frequently until golden brown.

Impossible Pies
Made with
Ham & Pork

Impossible Ham & Broccoli Casserole Pie

1 cup diced, fully cooked, smoked ham
3/4 cup chopped frozen broccoli, thawed & well drained
1 cup cooked white rice (use left-over rice if you have it*)
1/4 cup chopped onion
1 cup shredded Cheddar cheese (4 oz.)
1/2 cup Bisquick® baking mix
1 cup milk
2 large eggs
1/4 teaspoon salt
Pinch of ground black pepper

Preheat oven to 400°. Spray a 9" X 1-1/2" glass pie plate with cooking spray.

Stir together ham, broccoli, rice, onion and cheese. Spread mixture in pie plate.

In a small bowl, beat remaining ingredients together with a wire whisk until well blended. Pour into pie plate.

Bake about 35-40 minutes or until knife inserted in center comes out clean. Let stand 10 minutes before serving.

*Other recipes in this cookbook that call for cooked white rice: Sausage, Red Beans & Rice Pie (page 7), Tuna Polynesia Pie (page 26) and Pork Stroganoff Pie (page 32).

Impossible Pork & Hominy Pie

1 lb. ground pork
1/4 cup chopped onion
1 (15.5 oz.) can hominy, well drained
1 (4 oz.) can chopped green chilies, well drained
1/2 cup Bisquick® baking mix
1 cup milk
2 large eggs
1/4 teaspoon garlic powder
1/2 teaspoon salt
Pinch of ground black pepper

Preheat oven to 400°. Spray a 9" X 1-1/2" glass pie plate with cooking spray.

In a skillet, cook pork and onion until done; drain. Stir in hominy and green chilies and spread mixture in pie plate.

In a small bowl, beat remaining ingredients together with a wire whisk until well blended. Pour into pie plate.

Bake 35-40 minutes or until knife inserted in center comes out clean. Let stand 10 minutes before serving.

Serve warm with a tossed green salad or cool and crunchy Waldorf salad (mix chopped apple, celery and pecans with a little mayonnaise).

Impossible Scalloped Potato & Ham Pie

1 cup diced, fully cooked, smoked ham
1-1/2 cups cooked potato, peeled and diced*
1/2 cup finely chopped onion
1 cup shredded Cheddar cheese (4 oz.)
1/2 cup Bisquick® baking mix
1 cup milk
2 large eggs
1/2 teaspoon salt
Pinch of ground black pepper

Preheat oven to 400°. Spray a 9" X 1-1/2" glass pie plate with cooking spray.

Mix together ham, potato, onion and cheese and spread in pie plate.

In a small bowl, beat remaining ingredients together with a wire whisk until well blended. Pour into pie plate.

Bake about 35-40 minutes or until knife inserted in center comes out clean. Let stand 10 minutes before serving.

*Cook two medium potatoes in the microwave until soft. Let cool, then peel and dice.

Impossible Pork Tamale Pie

1 lb. ground pork
1/2 cup chopped onion
1/2 cup chopped, canned tomatoes (or Ro*Tel Tomatoes if
    you like it spicy), well drained
1/2 cup frozen corn, thawed and drained
1/2 cup Bisquick® baking mix
1/4 cup yellow cornmeal
1 teaspoon chili powder
1/2 teaspoon salt
1/4 teaspoon garlic powder
1 cup milk
2 large eggs

Preheat oven to 400°. Spray a 9" X 1-1/2" glass pie plate with cooking spray.

In a skillet, cook pork and onion until done; drain. Stir in tomatoes and corn. Spread mixture in pie plate.

In a small bowl, beat remaining ingredients together with a wire whisk until well blended. Pour into pie plate.

Bake 35-40 minutes or until knife inserted in center comes out clean. Let stand 10 minutes before serving.

Impossible Pork Stroganoff Pie

1 lb. ground pork
1/2 cup chopped onion
1 (6.5 oz.) can sliced mushrooms, well drained
1 cup cooked white rice (use left-over rice if you have it*)
1/2 cup Bisquick® baking mix
1/2 cup milk
1/2 cup sour cream
2 large eggs
1/4 teaspoon garlic powder
1/2 teaspoon salt
Pinch of ground black pepper

Preheat oven to 400°. Spray a 9" X 1-1/2" glass pie plate with cooking spray.

In a skillet, cook pork and onion until done; drain. Stir in mushrooms and rice. Spread mixture in pie plate.

In a small bowl, beat remaining ingredients together with a wire whisk until well blended. Pour into pie plate.

Bake 35-40 minutes or until knife inserted in center comes out clean. Let stand 10 minutes before serving.

*Other recipes in this cookbook that call for cooked white rice: Sausage, Red Beans & Rice Pie (page 7), Tuna Polynesia Pie (page 26) and Ham & Broccoli Casserole Pie (page 28).

Pies Made
with
Cheese &
Vegetables

Impossible Macaroni & Cheese Pie

1 cup uncooked elbow macaroni
2-1/2 cups shredded Cheddar cheese, divided
1/2 cup Bisquick® baking mix
3/4 cup milk
1/2 cup sour cream
1/2 teaspoon onion powder
1/2 teaspoon seasoned salt
1/8 teaspoon hot sauce (or to taste), optional
2 large eggs

Cook macaroni in boiling, salted water 5 minutes until just barely tender. Rinse and drain well.

Preheat oven to 400°. Spray a 9" X 1-1/2" glass pie plate with cooking spray.

Toss macaroni with 1-1/2 cups of cheese. Spread mixture in pie plate.

In a medium bowl, beat remaining ingredients together with a wire whisk until well blended. Pour into pie plate. Cover tightly with a sheet of foil.

Bake 25 minutes. Uncover and sprinkle with remaining 1 cup of cheese. Bake 5-10 minutes longer or until knife inserted in center comes out clean. Let stand at least 10 minutes before serving.

Impossible Fiesta Black Bean Pie

1 (15 oz.) can black beans, rinsed and drained
1 cup frozen corn, thawed and well drained
1/3 cup finely chopped onion
1 cup shredded Monterey Jack cheese (or Colby/Jack)
1/2 cup chunky salsa
1/2 cup Bisquick® baking mix
3/4 cup milk
2 large eggs
1/2 teaspoon salt
1/4 teaspoon garlic powder

Preheat oven to 400°. Spray a 9" X 1-1/2" glass pie plate with cooking spray.

Mix together beans, corn, onion, cheese and salsa. Spread in pie plate.

In a small bowl, beat remaining ingredients together with a wire whisk until well blended. Pour into pie plate.

Bake 35-40 minutes or until knife inserted in center comes out clean. Let stand 10 minutes before serving.

Serve warm with sour cream, chopped lettuce and tomato, and salsa, if desired.

Impossible Zucchini & Tomato Pie

2 cups diced zucchini
1 cup diced tomato, well drained
1/2 cup finely chopped onion
1 cup shredded Swiss cheese (or cheese of your choice)
3/4 cup Bisquick® baking mix
1-1/4 cups milk
3 large eggs
3/4 teaspoon salt
1/2 teaspoon dried thyme
Pinch of ground black pepper

Preheat oven to 400°. Spray a 9" X 1-1/2" glass pie plate with cooking spray.

Mix together zucchini, tomato, onion and cheese. Spread mixture in pie plate.

In a small bowl, beat remaining ingredients together with a wire whisk until well blended. Pour into pie plate.

Bake 45-50 minutes or until knife inserted in center comes out clean. Let stand at least 10 minutes before serving.

Impossible Green Bean Casserole Pie

1 (15 oz.) can French style green beans, well drained
1 cup canned French Fried Onions
1 (2 oz.) jar diced pimientos, well drained
1 (2 oz.) package sliced almonds (1/2 cup)*
1 cup shredded Cheddar cheese (4 oz.)
1/2 cup Bisquick® baking mix
1/2 cup milk
1/2 cup condensed cream of mushroom soup
2 large eggs
1 teaspoon Worcestershire sauce
1/4 teaspoon salt
Pinch of ground black pepper

Preheat oven to 400°. Spray a 9" X 1-1/2" glass pie plate with cooking spray.

Mix together beans, onions, pimientos, almonds and cheese. Spread mixture in pie plate.

In a small bowl, beat remaining ingredients together with a wire whisk until well blended. Pour into pie plate.

Bake 35-40 minutes or until knife inserted in center comes out clean. Let stand 10 minutes before serving.

*For added flavor, toast the almonds in a dry skillet over medium-high heat for 3-4 minutes, stirring frequently until golden brown.

Impossible Sweet Potato Casserole Pie

1 cup mashed, cooked and peeled sweet potatoes
    (canned sweet potatoes are fine)
1/2 cup chopped pecans
1/2 cup Bisquick® baking mix
1/2 cup brown sugar, packed
1 cup evaporated milk
2 large eggs
1 tablespoon butter or margarine, melted
1 teaspoon vanilla extract
1 teaspoon ground cinnamon

Preheat oven to 350°. Spray a 9" X 1-1/2" glass pie plate with cooking spray.

Beat all ingredients together, using a wire whisk or electric mixer, until well blended. Pour into pie plate.

Bake 35-40 minutes or until knife inserted in center comes out clean. Let stand 15 minutes before serving.

Optional: If you like marshmallows on top of your sweet potato casserole, sprinkle about 1 to 1-1/2 cups of miniature marshmallows on top of the pie after baking 30-35 minutes and return it to the oven for 5-10 minutes, until marshmallows are puffed and lightly browned.

Impossible
Dessert
Pies

Impossible Pecan Pie recipe

1-1/2 cups chopped pecans
3/4 cup milk
1/2 cup Bisquick® baking mix
4 large eggs
3/4 cup brown sugar, packed
3/4 cup corn syrup, light or dark
1/4 cup butter, melted
1 teaspoon vanilla extract

Preheat oven to 350°. Spray a 9" X 1-1/2" glass pie plate with cooking spray.

Sprinkle pecans into pie plate.

In a medium bowl, beat the remaining ingredients with an electric mixer until well blended. Pour into pie plate.

Bake 45-50 minutes or until knife inserted in center comes out clean. Let cool completely before serving.

Impossible Brownie Pie

4 large eggs
1/2 cup Bisquick® baking mix
1/4 c. butter or margarine, softened
4 (1 oz.) squares semi-sweet baking chocolate, melted & cooled
1/2 cup brown sugar, packed
1/2 cup granulated sugar
3/4 cup chopped pecans or walnuts

Preheat oven to 350°. Spray a 9" X 1-1/2" glass pie plate with cooking spray.

Beat all ingredients except nuts with an electric mixer until well blended.

Pour mixture into pie plate, sprinkle with nuts. Bake 35-40 minutes or until knife inserted in center comes out clean. Let cool completely before serving.

Impossible Lemon Custard Pie

1/4 cup butter or margarine, melted
4 large eggs
1 cup granulated sugar
1/2 cup Bisquick® baking mix
1 cup evaporated milk
3/4 cup lemon juice
1 teaspoon grated lemon zest

Preheat oven to 350°. Spray a 9" X 1-1/2" glass pie plate with cooking spray.

Place all ingredients in blender; cover and blend on high speed until smooth or place in a bowl and beat with an electric mixer or wire whisk until well blended. Pour into pie plate.

Bake 50-55 minutes or until a knife inserted in center comes out clean. Let cool and refrigerate several hours before serving.

Top each slice with sweetened whipped cream (recipe on page 43) or non-dairy whipped topping if desired.

Impossible Chocolate Cream Pie

2 large eggs
1 cup whole milk*
1/4 cup butter or margarine, melted
2 (1 oz.) squares unsweetened chocolate, melted
1 cup granulated sugar
1/2 cup Bisquick® baking mix

Preheat oven to 350º. Spray a 9" X 1-1/2" glass pie plate with cooking spray.

Place all ingredients in blender container; cover and blend on high about 1 minute. Or beat with a hand mixer until smooth. Pour batter into pie plate.

Bake 35-40 minutes or until knife inserted in center comes out clean. Let cool completely before serving. Top with sweetened whipped cream if desired.

Sweetened Whipped Cream: Beat 1 cup chilled whipping cream and 2 tablespoons granulated sugar with an electric mixer on high speed until stiff peaks form.

*If you don't have whole milk, substitute 1 cup skim milk plus 2 teaspoons melted butter or margarine.

Impossible Buttermilk Pie

1 cup granulated sugar*
1/2 cup Bisquick® baking mix
1 cup buttermilk
3 large eggs
1/3 cup butter or margarine, melted
1 teaspoon vanilla extract
1/8 teaspoon ground nutmeg (optional)

Preheat oven to 350°. Spray a 9" X 1-1/2" glass pie plate with cooking spray.

Beat all ingredients together until smooth, about 30 seconds in blender on high or 1 minute with electric mixer. Pour into pie plate.

Bake 35-40 minutes or until knife inserted in center comes out clean. Let cool completely before serving.

*If you like your buttermilk pie very sweet, increase the sugar to 1-1/2 cups.

Impossible Coconut Custard Pie

2 cups milk
4 large eggs
1/2 cup granulated sugar
1/2 cup Bisquick® baking mix
1 teaspoon vanilla extract
1/4 cup butter, melted
1/4 teaspoon salt
1 cup sweetened, flaked coconut, packed

Preheat oven to 350º. Spray a 9" X 1-1/2" glass pie plate with cooking spray.

Mix all ingredients together in a blender 1 minute or using an electric mixer 2 minutes or until smooth. Pour into pie plate.

Bake 45-50 minutes or until knife inserted into center comes out clean. Let cool completely before serving.

Impossible Cheesecake Pie

1/2 cup milk
1/2 cup sour cream
1 teaspoon vanilla extract
1 teaspoon lemon juice
3 large eggs
1 cup granulated sugar
1/2 cup Bisquick® baking mix
2 (8 oz.) packages cream cheese, softened

Preheat oven to 350º. Spray a 9" X 1-1/2" or 9.5" X 1-1/2" glass pie plate with cooking spray.

Using a blender or electric mixer, beat all ingredients together until well blended. Pour into pie plate. (Plate will be full, so make sure you are using a deep-dish pie plate for this recipe.)

Bake 45-50 minutes until the pie is set. Let cool and refrigerate several hours before serving.

Top each slice with cherry pie filling if desired.

Impossible Pumpkin Pie

1 cup canned pumpkin
1/2 cup Bisquick® baking mix
1 cup evaporated milk
2 large eggs
1 tablespoon margarine or butter, melted
1/2 cup brown sugar, packed
1-1/2 teaspoons pumpkin pie spice*
1 teaspoon vanilla extract

Preheat oven to 350°. Spray a 9" X 1-1/2" glass pie plate with cooking spray.

Beat all ingredients together with an electric mixer or wire whisk until thoroughly blended. Pour into pie plate.

Bake 35-40 minutes or until knife inserted in center comes out clean.

Let cool completely before serving.

*To make your own pumpkin pie spice, stir together 1 teaspoon ground cinnamon, 1/2 teaspoon ground nutmeg and 1/2 teaspoon ground ginger. Makes 2 teaspoons of spice mix.

Impossible Apple Pie

Apple Filling:
1 (20 oz.) can sliced apples, well drained
1 teaspoon ground cinnamon
1/2 cup Bisquick® baking mix
1/2 cup granulated sugar
1/2 cup milk
1 tablespoon butter or margarine, softened
2 large eggs

Streusel Topping:
1/2 cup Bisquick® baking mix
1/4 cup chopped pecans
1/4 cup brown sugar, packed
2 tablespoons butter or margarine, chilled

Preheat oven to 350°. Spray a 9" X 1-1/2" glass pie plate with cooking spray.

Toss apple slices with cinnamon and spread in pie plate.

Beat remaining filling ingredients together with a wire whisk until well blended. Pour into pie plate.

Stir together all streusel ingredients until crumbly. Sprinkle over apples. Bake 45 to 50 minutes or until knife inserted in center comes out clean. Let stand at least 15 minutes before serving.

Impossible Peaches & Cream Pie

Peach Filling:
1 (29 oz.) can sliced peaches, well drained
1/2 teaspoon ground cinnamon
2/3 cup Bisquick® baking mix
3/4 cup granulated sugar
1 cup heavy cream (or evaporated milk)
2 large eggs

Streusel Topping:
1/4 cup Bisquick® baking mix
1/4 cup chopped pecans (or slivered almonds)
2 tablespoons granulated sugar
1 tablespoon butter or margarine, chilled

Preheat oven to 350°. Spray a 9" X 1-1/2" glass pie plate with cooking spray.

Spread peaches in pie plate.

Beat remaining filling ingredients together with a wire whisk until well blended. Pour into pie plate.

Stir together all streusel ingredients until crumbly. Sprinkle over peaches. Bake 45 to 50 minutes or until knife inserted in center comes out clean. Cool completely before serving.

Other Books by Gloria Hander Lyons

- *Easy Microwave Desserts in a Mug*
- *Easy Microwave Desserts in a Mug for Kids*
- *No Rules – Just Fun Decorating*
- *Just Fun Decorating for Tweens & Teens*
- *Decorating Basics: For Men Only*
- *Ten Common Home Decorating Mistakes & How to Avoid Them*
- *If Teapots Could Talk—Fun Ideas for Tea Parties*
- *The Super-Bride's Guide for Dodging Wedding Pitfalls*
- *Lavender Sensations: Fragrant Herbs for Home & Bath*
- *A Taste of Lavender: Delectable Treats with an Exotic Floral Flavor*
- *Designs That Sell: How to Make Your Home Show Better & Sell Faster*
- *Self-Publishing on a Budget: A Do-It-All-Yourself Guide*
- *The Secret Ingredient: Tasty Recipes with an Unusual Twist*
- *Hand Over the Chocolate & No One Gets Hurt: The Chocolate-Lover's Cookbook*
- *Flamingos, Poodle Skirts & Red Hots: Creative Theme Party Ideas*
- *Quick Gifts From the Kitchen: No Cooking Required*
- *A Taste of Memories: Comforting Foods From Our Past*

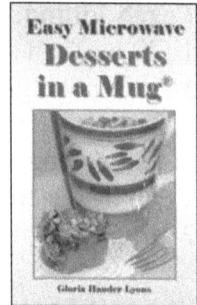

Easy Microwave
Desserts
in a Mug®

Gloria Hander Lyons

Index

About the Author

Gloria Hander Lyons has channeled 30 years of training and hands-on experience in the areas of art, interior decorating, crafting and event planning into writing creative how-to books. Her books cover a wide range of topics including decorating your home, cooking, planning weddings and tea parties, crafting and self-publishing.

Gloria has designed original craft projects featured in magazines, such as *Better Homes and Gardens, McCall's, Country Handcrafts* and *Crafts*. She teaches interior decorating, wedding planning and self-publishing classes at her local community college. Much to her family's delight, her kitchen is in non-stop test mode, creating recipes for new cookbooks.

Visit her website for free craft ideas, decorating and event planning tips and tasty recipes at: www.BlueSagePress.com.

Ordering Information

To order additional copies of this book, send check or money order payable to:

> Blue Sage Press
> 48 Borondo Pines
> La Marque, TX 77568

Cost for this edition is $6.95 per book (U.S. currency only) plus $3.00 shipping and handling for the first book and $1.25 for each additional book shipped to the same U.S. address. Texas residents add 8.25% sales tax to total order amount.

To pay by credit card or get a complete list of books written by Gloria Hander Lyons, visit our website:

www.BlueSagePress.com

www.ingramcontent.com/pod-product-compliance
Lightning Source LLC
Chambersburg PA
CBHW060614030426
42337CB00018B/3062